SYSTEM OF GHOSTS

Winner of the Iowa Poetry Prize

SYSTEM
OF GHOSTS

POEMS BY

LINDSAY TIGUE

University of Iowa Press ▪ Iowa City

University of Iowa Press, Iowa City 52242

www.uiowapress.org

Printed in the United States of America

Design by Barbara Haines

The University of Iowa Press is a member of Green Press Initiative and is committed to preserving natural resources.

Printed on acid-free paper

Library of Congress Cataloging-in-Publication Data
Names: Tigue, Lindsay.
Title: System of ghosts / Lindsay Tigue.
Description: Iowa City: University of Iowa Press, 2016.
Identifiers: LCCN 2015033811 | ISBN 978-1-60938-401-2 (pbk) | ISBN 978-1-60938-402-9 (ebk)
Classification: LCC PS3620.I485 A6 2016 | DDC 811/.6—dc23
LC record available at http://lccn.loc.gov/2015033811

■ *For my parents* ■

All American cities began at the end of something: a trail, a landing along a river or lake, a railroad.

—*American Urban Form: A Representative History*, Sam Bass Warner and Andrew H. Whittemore

Contents

III.

Acknowledgments

Thanks to the editors of the literary journals where some of these poems first appeared: "Adapted," *Adroit Journal*; "Linear Foreign Bodies," *Barnstorm*; "Elevator," "Millions," *Blackbird*; "For the Ghost You Might Become," "Solitary, Imaginary," *burntdistrict*; "E-How," "Neighbors," *Codex Journal*; "We are a System of Ghosts II," "We are a System of Ghosts III," "We are a System of Ghosts IV," *CutBank*; "Interview Practice," "Little Grand Canyon in Yellow," *diode*; "My Dad's Brother Called Every Year for Five Years Then Disappeared," *Drunken Boat*; "Drop," *Hayden's Ferry Review*; "Directions," *Hollins Critic*; "Michigan Central Station Has Been Closed Since 1988," *Indiana Review*; "Needs Assessment," *Iron Horse Literary Review*; "Canopic Jars," "Frontier Airlines," "Strange Ducks," *The Literary Review*; "Abandoned Places," *Ninth Letter Online*; "Convergent Boundaries," *Passages North*; "Abandoned Places," *The Pinch*; "We are a System of Ghosts I," *Poet Lore*; "Bliss," *Prairie Schooner*; "The Trajectory of Oranges," *Puerto del Sol Online*; "New Year," *Rattle*; "How to Care for Buffalo Horns," *RealPoetik*.

"The Center of the Earth is a Little Off Kilter," "To Disappear in Michigan," and "Huron" originally appeared in *Prairie Gold: An Anthology of the American Heartland*.

So much thanks to colleagues, faculty, and friends at the University of Georgia, Iowa State University, Michigan State University, the Sewanee Writers' Conference, the Great Books Foundation, Sundress Academy for the Arts, the Rensing Center, the Literary Writers' Network in Chicago, and StoryStudio Chicago. Thanks to the University of Iowa Press and Craig Morgan Teicher. I would like to especially thank Debra Marquart, Mary Swander, Brianna Burke, Kimberly Zarecor, Stephen Pett, Benjamin Percy, Dean Bakopoulos, David Zimmerman, K. L. Cook, Maurice Manning, Rick Bass, Baird Harper, Magdalena Zurawski, Andrew Zawacki, Ed Pavlić, LeAnne Howe, Reginald McKnight, Shamala Gallagher, Adam Gardner,

Caroline Young, Gale Marie Thompson, Gabrielle Lucille Fuentes, Thibault Raoult, Sara Renee Marshall, Gina Abelkop, Kristen Gleason, Jenny Gropp, Tegan Swanson, Walker Pett, Tony Quick, Logan Adams, Liz Giorgi, Andrew Payton, Lindsay D'Andrea, Geetha Iyer, Sarah Burke, Xavier Cavazos, Michelle Donahue, Chris Wiewiora, Anya Groner, Seth Sawyers, Christen Enos, Emma Duffy-Comparone, Cara Blue Adams, Josh Robbins, Liz Zabel, Jim Porter, Deborah Miller, Daniel Born, Peter Ho Davies, Diane Wakoski, W. S. Penn, Marcia Aldrich, Richard Swartout, Alison Keller, Kristin Lord, Joshua Lord, Emily Birchmeier, Julia Slocum, Lonna Nachtigal, Joe Lynch, Molly Benningfield, Ashley Cheuk, Ruth Mowry, Lindsey Kate Sloan, Jill Kolongowski, Margot Kielhorn, Teal Amthor-Shaffer, and Kate Anderson.

Thank you to my Tigue and Anderson families. I love you all so much.

To Nancy, Dave, Alyssa, and A. J. Your support is everything to me.

I.

MILLIONS

There were uncounted millions of the beasts—hundreds of millions,
we forced ourselves to believe.   —Frank H. Mayer,
                                        The Buffalo Harvest

I *can't* force myself to believe in any old
                                almanac, that the best days for fishing
            will come mid-March, that fog in January
                                        brings a wet spring.

Most of my knowledge gets turned, or upset. Even chickens
                aren't completely flightless—they can make it
                        over a fence, into the low branches
of trees. In China, a man built his own dialysis machine, kept
                                himself alive for thirteen years.

Wolverines will rescue people from snowbanks, dragging them
                by their shirtsleeves to safety.

At the Maeklong Railway Market in Thailand, tourists marvel
                                        eight times a day
                    at produce stalls set right on the tracks,
whole shops removed as a train barges through.

Like clockwork, the market reassembles. I always question
            the most rigid convictions. I can't trust a person
                    who plays the lottery, believes in planning

for luck. I think someone evil once said, *a single death
                is a tragedy, a million a statistic.* I don't buy into
the claptrap of despots. I want to say the word *miracle* somehow
                                without cringing, believe
types of goodness exist. Oh. It's too easy
to trust—
            the future arrives; the honeymoon happens.
                    The baby is born with ten fingers, ten toes.

DIRECTIONS

Call it knowledge—
wanting to see

how the world is made.
My new roommate goes to the store,

buys crystals, practices archery
in the backyard. The arrows fly

toward our house, a still-new
place. Sometimes I forget

how to recycle batteries,
to not undress

in front of open windows at night. One
summer, when I worked at a park,

visitors brought ashes. They carried
urns, wanting to leave people

in the mountains. One man walked
along the road, tipped out

his canister right on the guardrail.
Ashes sat there for days, so bone-white

in the rain. I wouldn't clear them away.
I can be energy and wait.

Is this a particular missing? I am
no longer by the mountains. No

longer by plains. The other day I
dreamed of the person I might

miss most. He was dressed like
a cell-phone salesman. He put his nose

to my cheek. The other day, I asked
my phone for directions to a place.

I didn't go. All day, a voice called out: *Turn left.*

SOLITARY, IMAGINARY

At our new house, empty scrap
framed weedy earth, but my mother said:
a perfect sandbox.

The sand came from a store, but I still hoped
to find a shell, the smell of sea,
some smooth-edged bottle glass sifted
from dunes.

I'd drag lines in the mineral grain
with my plastic rake. I'd dream
summer on Hampton Beach, New Hampshire's
thin eyelash of coast.

I'd remember burying my limbs,
how I splashed steps into waves. How I
called my imaginary plans:
I'll chase the water out until it's gone.

These days, I live alone
and sit near a computer. All day,
I stare. And when the electricity goes out
with its slapped silence,

I act like I'm not thrilled, that I don't love
to meet neighbors in the street. *Do you
have power?* I ask. *Do you have light?*

HOW TO ADJUST TO TIME ZONES

When the Union Pacific
and the Central Pacific
formed one railroad, more
than 8,000 towns
used local time.

Before the railroad,
people based time
on the natural
movement of the sun.

Now, my sister lives
two hours behind me.
My brother one hour
ahead.

In the 1870s, railroads
created bureaus, sent agents
east, to Europe, attracting
settlers to this land.

Hold your eyelids
wide open with your fingers. Go
outdoors as much as possible.
Natural light will reset
your body's clock. Retire to sleep
at the local bedtime.

CITY OF LIGHT

> Everything—houses, churches, bridges, walls—is the same sandy gray so that the city seems like a single construction of inconceivable complexity.
>
> —Rebecca Solnit,
> *Wanderlust: A History of Walking*

Do you remember the front door
painted blue? How it even rained,
but we stayed in the Hotel Perfect.
At the tower, they wouldn't let us go up
to the top, only the near-top. And you
patted the beams, joked about structural
integrity. *I've never seen a place like this,*
you said. Do you still remember
my terrible French? Coming back
from Versailles, we couldn't wait to peel
those rain-soaked clothes. I can't be sure—
all my you-memories become one
sprawling city. Was it on that trip
you mimicked the poses of statues
we saw in the park? On a different trip,
(that night it snowed), we stopped
at an Indiana motel, drank a bottle
of wine naked, dripping on sheets.
I stayed there again once, alone.
Out the window, cars rumbled away.
It rained and the power went out.
The building noises silenced
with drawn-out whirs like breaths.

THE TRAJECTORY OF ORANGES

All night, in the train car to Valencia, the young couple speaks
Italian, propped on elbows in their bunks. Their whispered

joy hovers like a tent. They are a skylight above me. I catch words,
snatches of sense. I am teenaged and thrilled

by history. Now, the couple peels oranges—one, then another,
another. They citrus-fill the compartment with noise

and snack. They hand slices near the ceiling; they drop rinds
like shed chrysalis, like discarded drafts, like we may

all become new before long. I may never think beyond
oranges again—their smell sharpens the air. Perhaps

we are like explorers bringing fruit to Iberia, we travelers,
like royalty. We are Europe in the 17th century. Citriculture

is for kings. Or, we speak Middle English, rename this color
after crop. There is no longer yellow-red. Let us navigate,

crating seedlings across an ocean from Spain. In Bahia, we'll celebrate
the birth of navel oranges. It looks like *umbigo*, we'll say. The button

of my belly. Who ate the first orange? The new hybrid of mandarin
and pummelo, in that corner confluence of India, China, Burma,

whatever land was there then. This taste for new food—maybe
I carry memories in my tongue. *I am young, too*, I could tell them

and can I be like you? I will speak citrus. I will claw at the peels.
The train roars across track and I want orange dust near this skin.

BLISS

A motor vehicle carries us to our graves.

—Clay McShane,
*The Automobile: A Chronology of Its Antecedents,
Development, and Impact*

You know, they had traffic
in ancient Rome and in 1769,
Nicolas Cugnot built a steam-powered

gun carriage. He ran it into a wall.
In 1899, in New York City, Arthur Smith
hit H. H. Bliss, the first American pedestrian

killed by car. I don't like to pilot,
steer. And I don't want to drive
you home. Did you know

the word *cab* comes from
cabriolet? My grandmother
made me sit in the backseat.

Precious cargo, she called me,
rolling slowly over dirt roads.
Each pothole borne in my bones.

In 1817, streets were still
meeting places. I want to remember
the first streetlights, the ideas for green

and red borrowed from passing ships.
I see us entering the earliest crosswalk,
the semaphore arm raised. And later—

illuminated at night—those fog-edged
boxes glowing instruction. We can't even
trust ourselves to look both ways.

ABANDONED PLACES

The house on sinking Holland Island—
an old Victorian, shingles-crumbling,

the isle's last structure falling into
the Chesapeake Bay.

Before it collapsed in 2010,
one couple rowed out there.

I click through their photos—
the house's interior full of dusty

bottles, broken furniture. Their shots
of gulls in flight. A rusty tub. Their GPS

to guide them. They walked through
the island's old cemetery, from its days

as village, where watermen lived
and dredged oysters in the bay.

The land has been sinking
for thousands of years. The water

rising ever more quickly. In
2003, hurricane waves rushed

through the kitchen. This place
of silt and clay knows how

to disappear. In 1995, one man
bought the island and wanted

to save it himself. The experts said
he never had a chance. He tried

building breakwaters out of wood.
He put down hundreds of sandbags,

lined large rocks against the shoreline.
Before it fell, that house appeared

to sit directly on the waves. The man
gave up the island after he turned

eighty, underwent chemotherapy.
The couple's photos online show

his favorite grown-over headstone,
a girl's grave that reads: *Forget me not*

is all I ask.

ADAPTED

The Blackfoot of the Plains had over
a hundred words for the colors
of horses, their many varied,
running shades. If only we could all
be as reliable as the horses we rode in on.
I want many words for you. I want
something as far as I can throw it. No,
farther. You say, I throw like a girl. I do
everything that way. I ask, is the flue
open and you look up the chimney. I ask,
can you see the sky? Can we have
heat? Before you walk away, try to find it.
Fix the dripping radiator. Don't travel
too far—walk, or ride out on some
journey alone. Our brains too big
for our bodies, too big for the cage
of our skeleton. Even our bipedal
nature changed everything. The bones
in our feet rearranged. This whole house
smells of body. Damp shower and sheet.
I show you my socks that are starting to thin
and you say, *here come the toes.* I point to our
curtains falling from window. You won't
fix it all before you go.

LITTLE GRAND CANYON IN YELLOW
—at the Georgia Museum of Art

The teenagers stare at the canvas.
At the art museum, I watch them
squirm with body-newness, struggle
with attention. The curator shows
a Howard Thomas painting. Providence
Canyon in color. Orange. Red. Yellow.
Anything, but everything warm. Thomas
used earth pigments. Grinding up soil,
mixing for color. Quaker-born, from Ohio,
during his first trip to the South, he
gathered red clay outside Asheville.

In the museum, in a Lucite case,
I see the baby food jars of his color
collection. Labeled—detailed records,
natural materials. The jar lids instruct,

Twist. When I first arrived in the South,
I stayed in the very same mountains.
I spent the summer in a camper
with a man who understood newness,
who once buried his documents, his identity
in the ground, changed his name. Spent
time in jail for it, hidden, staring I suppose
at some wall blankness. He told me, *I think
I might love you*. I didn't say anything
back. At the museum, the curator explains

Thomas's process. She says it was like dancing.
That he placed the canvas on the floor. He
played music in the background. Bach,
Vivaldi, Haydn. She closes her eyes to what

she might hear. She begins to hop about
the gallery, she dabs invisible paint

across the floor. The teenagers
stare. One boy asks, *What does it mean?*
After they leave, I approach
the jars. I imagine someone asks, *have you
been there?*

The other day, a new friend walked
along the river, uncovered an old homestead.
She found clouded milk
glass, dusty vessels, broken cans.

A few hours south, the ground.
I've learned it gapes open. I didn't know
there were canyons. Here. And somewhere:
caves. Somehow: a way to read
colors. The rows of jars that
have to mean something.

ELEVATOR

She's forgotten to call
her mother. Stayed in bed

hours too long. She's left
the garden's tomatoes

to rot. She's woken up,
still loving the wrong

man. Of course, she's forgotten
to eat. Then later, shaking,

she's plied the near-empty
vending machine with coins. She's taken

whatever she can get. Today, she's gone
to an office, sat at a desk.

Head pounding, left eye twitching.
She's taken pills to calm

the thrumming skull. Today,
leaving, a young man has stuck his hand

in the closing door of the elevator.
I'm sorry, she's said. As if she was

supposed to know he was coming.
I'm sorry, she's said. *Do*

you want to know a secret?
he's said out of nowhere. *Sure.*

He's told her he's pushed the alarm button
over and over. It has rung

many times in her head.
Nothing will happen, he's told her.

No one will come. The elevator door
has opened onto a room of desks.

Suited people have raised their heads
from documents and screens.

Yesterday, at group therapy,
she was made to repeat:

I am worthy. She's had to do
this every week. She thought it

stupid until it wasn't.
Maybe next time after saying it—

I am worthy—she'll remember the faces
beyond the elevator. Their asking: *who*

is sounding this alarm?

II.

WE ARE A SYSTEM OF GHOSTS

i.

is what a man says in a documentary about his city.
At least, that's what I remember he says. When I rewind

to find his words, I'm not surprised that I can't. Once,
before I lived there, my mother brought me to Chicago

and we laughed through downtown like girls.
We drank wine and ate pasta. A few years later,

we tried to find it again, this best-ever place,
but we'd forgotten the sidewalk to turn down, or the way

the restaurant's awning threw its door frame in shadow.
My mother protested: *but these streets are a grid.*

She studied the map pressed flat to her knees. I think of all the maps
of countries and borders that no longer exist. In France,

I lived near the site of the Ligne Maginot, that line of tankers
and casements in World War II designed to keep Germany out—

the countryside dotted with armored cloches of alloyed steel.
The machine-gun turrets retracting into the ground. This vanishing

reminds me of informal cities, the claimed settlements
that appear along abandoned rail tracks, the spaces people fill

and empty. The woman in the apartment below me has birds
and they squawk in greeting when they see her, as if to say:

oh there you are. I listen as her front door slams each day. Maybe
she watches as I wait for the bus, my eyes shut tight to the wind.

ii.

I once saw a photo of someone stranded
in an Iowa blizzard, a figure covered in flurry—

the white, sleeting lines erasing all edges of body.
Hopper-solitary in the flatness. A year later,

I couldn't even begin to locate it in a book
or museum, couldn't remember anything at all except

snow. Most days, half the mail I get is for others.
Or, it isn't even addressed to a name:

Current Resident. I pile it all in a shoebox and keep it
up, away on a shelf. Most days, I want to research

a trip somewhere new. I look up the logistics,
the to and from: the airport, the taxis, the buses,

and trains. I will always know what to do
if I get there. I want to go somewhere

that requires goggles to protect my eyes
against snow blindness, to avoid flash burns

of the cornea. They say it's like an eyeful of sand.
Do I enjoy the feeling of standing in a field,

full of it, alone? Polar explorers treated
this exposure with drops of cocaine in their eyes.

I research that, too. Visitors to Antarctica still arrive
by sea, on a boat from Ushuaia, the southern tip

of Argentina. Thousands of people go each year,
wanting to witness that which disappears. I see them

trekking over ice. On my daily walks home, it's not
winter yet and I can only retrieve what's fallen—I collect

buckeyes, pinecones, horseapples, walnuts. I fold
and store leaves like small paper receipts.

iii.

The moving trucks all came on the same day.
In Lakewood, California, in 1950, a new suburb began.

I imagine the trucks unloading, their leaving,
unpacking. People in new structures:

here we are. In the 1950s, single-family homes diffused
on treeless plots near highway.   So many residents

could wake up and feel: *nowhere*. In an Iowa coffee shop,
on the edge of once-prairie, I write long

overdue letters to friends. A little girl approaches,
sticks her head in my lap. She taps a key on my laptop.

She types a series of O's. *This is a ghost story*, she says.
Is it scary? I want to know.   She types *EEEEE*.

I ask: *is somebody screaming?*

iv.

On the bus, I read about Japan's suicide forest.
Aokigahara, near the base of Mount Fuji.

People say it's the best place to die.
They tie rope along trunks, a trail for whomever

comes after. The bodies get cleared out once a year
by volunteers and officials. Park ranger Azusa Hayano

has talked hundreds of people out of their plans.
He's rescued so many half-dying already.

Hayano puts a hand on their shoulder.
He asks them to speak as they sit near the trees.

CONVERGENT BOUNDARIES

Isostatic sinking is caused by heavy weight,
as during glaciation, the lowering of crust
into asthenosphere. I read about this process,
involved in the creation of atolls, coral necklace
landmass ringing bluewater lagoon.

I tell you *this* is my new favorite
geologic event. That I also love
subduction, when one tectonic plate sinks
below the other at convergent boundaries,
causing hot magma to rise to the surface.

When I told you about subduction,
I slipped, said seduction. That's what
this is. But you know that.

In fifth grade, when I first learned
about the rift of Pangaea, I cried.
It was too beautiful, the way everything can
and will separate.

But what about love that is there, my god
it is there, but can't seem to force
the shifting of what's already in place,
the fault-line fissure, continents halving
into sea. The division of everything—
records and cups and quilts. You can't see

how the dust might settle. I keep
wanting my own sinking, your reckless weight
above me. Your hand on my back. The ring
of myself that remains.

HOW TO CARE FOR BUFFALO HORNS

And all we had to do was take these hides from their wearers.
It was a harvest. We were the harvesters.

> —Frank H. Mayer,
> *The Buffalo Harvest*

You will need:
    a soft cloth
    linseed oil
    car wax
    an air canister.
You will need buffalo horns.

Buffalo were shot
for sport, men hanging
out train car windows.

A Kiowa woman remembered
a pile of bones as tall as a man
and a mile long, ready
to ship to eastern markets.

They say the buffalo used
to block the tracks
a thousand strong. That once
an impatient conductor
fired at a herd. They stampeded,
derailed his train.

So, wipe the horns of dust
and debris. Apply linseed oil.
Let it soak. Apply car wax
with your fingertips
in a circular motion.
Finish by dusting
with compressed air.

HISTORY OF ROOMS

i.

My earliest memory is spatial—
the vague layout of a home.
I can almost see
the way the hallway towered
and turned. I was two
when we moved, but learning
to walk, I swear
I palmed the walls.

Other interiors are full
of chalk dust, faux-marbled tile,
announcements scrolled on a ticker. *Sign
up. Field day. Go Wolves. Blood Drive. Bake
Sale.* When I drive past middle school
now, they've torn down half. Gone
are the rows of green lockers,
thick with decades of paint, coated
in kelly drips dried on metal doors.
And the band room, where I sat, unable
to breathe the measures. Gone the stale carpet,
soaked in my spit.

ii.

I could make a map
and a paper doll me and I
could place this me into paper-doll rooms
from long-ago years and
every room means a smell. Swedish pancake
smell here. Irish coffee smell
here. Noxzema smell. Hairspray smell.
Detergent smell upstairs.

iii.

In France, I got close
to my blue-tiled floor,
where I lived above the cantine.
I'd listen to lunchtime—
the chatter of students, the din
of fork and knife.

iv.

The man I loved
lined card tables end to end
in his Chicago apartment,
draped it with a bedsheet.
He placed a large votive candle on
his makeshift tablecloth. We had
iceberg salad, steak in the pasta. We broke
bread next to the radiator
breathing winter heat.

ABANDONED PLACES

So maybe I am a town
for ghosts. And I know that
places can fall in love

with those who stay awhile,
those who sweep the cracking
stairs, repair the panes

on all the windows. In the Sierras,
on the border between Nevada
and California sits Bodie—its decaying

wood and still-stocked stores.
In my mind, these towns,
are never empty—their rail

lines coming and going
through mountains and plains.
When he left me, I guess

I didn't think about nowhere.
The dim promise of gold.
The park ranger in Bodie

gets cursed souvenirs returned
to him by mail. Contraband—
an old nail. A shard of glass. *I'm sorry,*

the notes say. *For what I've taken.*
I don't believe I fall for just
anyone who shows me kindness.

MICHIGAN CENTRAL STATION HAS BEEN CLOSED SINCE 1988

When I go visit you on the edge of an actual mountain in Colorado, we take the cog railway to the top. Toothed rack rail that jerks and chugs. We pay thirty dollars to go up and down and the grade steepens and a baby cries grabbing her ears, but we pass some of the oldest trees on earth— ancient bristlecone pines I know we'll forget. Past timberline, the train inches and I wait to roller coaster up and away from here, but we reach the top and the conductor says, *forty minutes!*, points to a concession stand selling nachos and we hate nachos. *But you love trains*, you say and I tell you I do. That night, we eat at Pizza Junction in an old sleeper car. The food isn't great like we want it to be and I touch the wall's wood paneling and ask you why can't all the stations become train stations again? And you say, while we're at it, let the mountains be mountains.

A week later, I leave you and fly home in the dark to find spilled vinegar in the kitchen and, for a moment, think it is blood. I sit on the floor looking at the stain I'll have to scrub best-I-can from the linoleum and I stare at the guilty cat as he jumps from counter to floor and stumbles his landing and licks his leg. I love to catch an animal pretending.

That night, I don't even tell you I'm home. I leave my packed suitcase on my bed, unlock my bicycle, and ride toward empty tracks, toward the nail salon in the old depot. I look for hills—Midwestern land isn't as flat when I'm pedaling. I wish I could bike all the way to Detroit, to the old abandoned station that looks like the end of time. You once told me that in 1912 it was the tallest rail station in this world, that it was modeled after ancient Roman bathhouses. I stop in front of Happy Nail Spa where a woman sits in the dark sanitizing clippers and I stand over my bike and pick up a discarded pop can, shake dirt on the toe of my shoe and try to remember the last time our faces touched. I watch the sign's fluorescent "N" flicker and buzz and I dream up trains flashing past me and I see all those passengers like ghosts crowding the station. I see people rushing in and out of a place. At all hours of any day.

FOR THE GHOST YOU MIGHT BECOME

Stand always too close. Become misplaced
as you need to be. You must wall
yourself in an old streaked phone booth,
run yourself against its wires spilling
to nowhere. You should roll a wagon
over gravel with a child inside, her hands
clasping a pail sloshing water over
stones. Rake your palm through tree rot.
Rub its umber matter against your shins.
Seek silence that fills with pine trunk creak.
And after you settle in this shifting, lose
largeness. Lose any sense of it at all.

LEAP

At age twelve:
during a class trip to the aquarium, I took
photo after photo. The trainer threw food
to the dolphins. She called them by name.
I pressed the shutter, almost
maniacally. I wanted to capture
their air. All of my photos appeared far away.
My mother asked me *why*—a whole
roll of grainy dolphin-leaps, these distant specks
above too-green water.
She stacked the blurry images
on my nightstand; I flipped through them
like flash cards—jump,
jump. All the arrested
arcs, the gray floating
animals in leap.

Tonight:
kids bike summer circles in the dark
outside my window.
They're making plans.
We can go there, they say. *But it's a long way.*

TO DISAPPEAR IN MICHIGAN

The cougar has been considered officially extinct in Michigan since 1906, although the animal has been spotted there with amazing frequency over the years.
—National Wildlife Federation, 2003

In Kalkaska County at midnight, some creature lurks
and crawls. The quiet farm waits in the pause
before growl. The silence pools into land—

out toward holes where glaciers notched the fresh sea.
In that water, where we killed all grayling and cisco fish—
Blackfin, Longjaw, Deepwater, Shortnose—where we still

look for glimmers of schools; images, blurry,
swimming from hooks. But in Kalkaska, a beast
believed gone, bloodies a family dog behind a barn. We lose

chickens one by one, examining teeth marks on their necks.
New days mark new death. And in the early fog, we
discover claw-streaked tracks of pain scraped in a mule.

Some cat's shadow fleets through woods. There are ways
this story must go. And when we learn the missing hometown
girl—fourteen—was found in California, we cannot believe

somewhere she breathes. That she fought
to vanish. That she wished to run
away. We only want her back—wouldn't you

miss these inland waters, these waves persisting
in their creep toward shore? The image of a cat caught
slipping out of woods—we don't have to see it. We know

how it looks. We think we know what breathes. What's
breathing? We can see exhaled air at night. We know
what happens behind barns, inside bedrooms, under a sea.

MY DAD'S BROTHER CALLED EVERY YEAR
FOR FIVE YEARS THEN DISAPPEARED

In Washington, human feet
Wash up on beaches, sneakers
With remains inside. I imagine a waterlogged
Mush of skin, bones. In eleven months—six feet
In buoyant rubber-soled trainers, tiny digits
Tucked safely. Not fish food. Like an omen,
A warning, we'll theorize, wanting signs to float in.
The news keeps reporting such mysteries.
For it's as if we're all waiting for bodies.

Look for company. Shuffle through wind,
Torn. Uncle, we saw you. You lived here once,
Drunk, filled with brittle plans. You were all
Under a spell. Your daughter, she spoke to you
Clasped and hurt, examining your chin
Before you died. Family gave you
Pieces. People wish you sent something back.
We'd watch for you in places, my dad pacing.
Be quiet, he'd whisper. *Eric's on the phone.*

STRANGE DUCKS

Before Cousin Tim's service,
my father scared away ducks.
In his funeral suit, he stood
on the deck yelling *get out of here,*
or *leave if you know what's good for you.*
From beyond the window, it was as if
he danced, sang mutely at the lake.

At Tim's house, stacked cut wood
ran the length of the porch.
At the funeral, I wanted fewer songs
about angel's wings because I don't
believe in angels. Least of all their wings.

The week before I'd wondered why
don't I know more? The Romans
built aqueducts to carry water
from the source. Why can't I
hang curtains that won't fall down?

Tim was handy. He built his own roof.
His wife described him finishing in the dark.
How he waited for passing cars. How he
worked in their flashes of vanishing light.

At the church, above the priest,
Jesus' arms display painted drips.
Every week, people look up
at this bleeding and isn't that funny?
Not funny ha-ha. And is it not crazy
to fly in a plane, starting in Michigan
and ending in Iowa? I tell my friend: *I feel
so strange.*

I feel light, too, and when, my friend
retrieves me from the airport in Iowa
he says: *Isn't it weird*
that we mention the dead?
Isn't it odd how we call them
by name?

NEW YEAR

The man who photographed
the very first plane to hit
air was using a camera
for the very first time.
The Wright brothers never
married. Wilbur once said
he *did not have time for both*
a wife and an airplane.

I could put a husband,
a wife, or daughter in this poem.
You might think someone
was waiting for me to come
back home.

I spent the first day
of this new year
in Antigua, Guatemala,
queasy. Firecrackers exploded
near my feet, paper lanterns
rose toward sky.

At the end of the day,
I walked through
Antigua alone, saw a mass
of people in black. A funeral
march. The mourners held
photos, and flowers, crosses,
and signs. Slowly, they walked
through the streets.

CANOPIC JARS

We crawled into a submarine without speaking
at the Museum of Science and Industry
and in the model of a U-boat bunkroom, you
pointed to torpedoes stacked behind the tiered beds
where German soldiers slept in shifts.

We walked through an exhibit of bodies,
human flesh and muscles preserved forever
with polymers. In the gift shop, they sold keychains
of little plastic human organs. Those slices
of muscle we observed without comment,
our bodies in terrible clarity.

In a Paris museum, we saw the canopic jars
of Egyptians, their containers of mummified
viscera: the stomach, intestines, lungs, and liver
each in a vessel. They left the heart
right in the body. We saw those alabaster jars,
the tops shaped like heads of baboon,
human, jackal, and falcon.

Realizing we would never make it
was like learning about the globe's shifting
plates, the way the earth's floor still spreads
beneath sea. Or when I first heard the voices
of whales. Their calls through dark caverns of water.

I imagine our hearts left in Ball jars, stored
in a cabinet for winter. Not our human hearts,
our heart-shaped hearts. I want to create jars
for other hearts—ones as big, as impossible
as those of blue whales. Hearts as large
as a car could pulse against glass.

ABANDONED PLACES

It's not like I can decide
to feel differently but here
goes. Today, I stop at a gas
station. I remove my iced tea
from the cooler and notice
a voice. A man stocking
shelves from the other side.
Maybe I'm too close
to love you, he sings. Maybe so.
Today, I get emails from
my doctor's office. *How*
is your mood today? They
ask me to rate my feelings
on a scale. I email back
a number. In Chernobyl,
wolves have returned, roaming
the unpeopled streets. My friend
tells me this as if she knows
it's what I need to hear.

DROP

Drop what you're doing this instant. Drop
that melon, that mop. Let's get out
of here and fast. There's rust in the oven,
newspapers stacked on a stoop. There is
too much everywhere. Let's purge
this house of knickknacks, receipts. I don't
want to remember the missing. Most of all,
let me lose those stone-frozen eyes—
how the man I loved looked saying: *I
never really wanted you.* Too bad. Maybe
I'm already heading West, cutting
my car through night flatness, looking
for ghost stampedes, handfuls of beasts.

III.

FRONTIER AIRLINES

The end of this plane's wing
displays the image of a deer. The woman

next to me closes the shade
while passing above the Grand Canyon.

I think to tell her, *I want*
and *I want* and *I want.* No,

I repeat, *I love* and *I love*
and *I love.* In my hotel room,

there is artwork of pen scrawls
that look like a star. Next to it,

it says, *Navajo Blanket.*
I flew across the West

alone. I gathered
liquids in bags.

The woman at the gate
hadn't flown in twenty years.

Going to see a grandbaby.
In the hotel gym, people lifted

their legs to the music. I could be
somewhere.

At the end of the flight,
a man flung open overhead

bins. *Sir*, the attendants said. *Sir.*
This aircraft is moving.

THE CENTER OF THE EARTH IS A LITTLE OFF KILTER

is what the newspaper says in regard to Ecuador's
Middle of the World, the equatorial park
whose monument to midpoint is hundreds of feet
from actual zero. But I like a middle that isn't
quite. For I'm in Chicago and, at home
in this Midwest, I can't sleep through the night.
The trains pass and stop right beyond my wall
and I wake flinching, dreaming they might
                    rush right through the brick and plaster.

But the end of my night turns into beginning
of morning and in half-sleep, my thoughts always
meander. When Rome fell the Middle Ages began
and measurements started to wander. How much
is a gill? A gallon?
                    Can you give me half a pounce?

I used to babysit a girl who pressed loose
the coarse skin around my elbow as I read to her
stories before bed. It was as if she could polish
me like stone, like she could knead
toward the center of my arm. She'd bend
my free limb like a doctor. She'd watch my joint
                    disappear into crater.

In middle school, I gave a presentation
on radiometric dating, the half-life of rocks,
the methods used to age this world. And when I wake
from nightmares about mass extinctions—
bees vanishing in the dark, I hear only the slow buzz
                    of my lights turning on.

At my parents' wedding anniversary, my dad
stood up at the table, toasted a glass.
He said, *I've known you*
                more than half this life.

In Ecuador, tourists stand right on a yellow line
marking the not center. *Take my picture.* And when I notch
off days on my calendar, I think: we invented that, too.
I just can't tell you when morning began for I'm still
dreaming of elbows and bees. I'm just
                waiting for reasons to measure.

E-HOW

How does a network connect?
How will a train cross the country?
How can I know *here* what you know *there*?
Why must we know? What
do we know? Where does a train go
when it disappears in a mountain?
What is it like inside mountains?
Who answers my questions?
If I have a cough, a fever, and itchy elbows,
what does this mean?
What do I have if I have fifty-two dollars
in quarters, two Canadian pennies,
an overdue library book?
After the invention of telephones,
what was it like to speak with familiar
voices so many miles away?
When I type into the url bar,
why do I always forget where I'm going?
How does it work tin-can operator? What
is on the other end of these keys?
Why can't all exits be formal—
a train pulling away, a person
left at the station, an arm
frozen mid-wave?

HOW TO MEASURE THE WEIGHT OF SNOW

You will need:
    a ruler
    a shovel
    a bucket
    a scale.
You will need snow.

In the winter of 1866,
the Chinese railroaders
for the Central Pacific
built tunnels under snow
to keep laying track.
Entire crews trapped
under tons, left
until spring melt found them.
Picks and shovels in their hands.

I used to wait for a school bus
on top of a plow drift
taller than me, slush-grayed
and calcified.

I used to wonder how much
snow weighed, lying inside
hand-packed igloos in my yard.

Measure your bucket.
Measure the top surface
of snow where it's flat.
Carve out a square foot
from the earth.
Place snow in your bucket
and weigh
before melting.

After the snow-load roof collapse
of the Carolina Waterfowl Rescue,
birds were injured, frozen solid.

I listen to the silent buildup
of snow on my peaked roof
until I can't hear it anymore.
Only the slow scraping
of a shovel clears the way outside.

As the birds melted, they tried
to open their mouths, their eyes.

THE BODY TRAVELS

My last day of middle school: all
shaving cream—throwing, spraying,
scraping from eyes. We arrived
at Depot Park, cans of Barbasol
stowed in backpacks and shirts.
Chasing each other, the slides and swings
became coated in goop, our hair drying
in stiff sections, glazed
like still-wet papier-mâché.
The next day, the whole class
went to roller coasters. To the park
whose slogan promised feet flipped
in the air. A friend explained
why I skipped most rides: *She doesn't like
the feeling.* I worried this was true. I swore
to enjoy the racked incline
toward hill, the inversion,
my sneakers scissoring sky.

I keep a photo from that day
of myself and a classmate.
I barely knew him. We
wandered, took an old-fashioned photo
set in a silly Wild West saloon. I wear
a feather boa, hold a plastic pistol
in my hand. He grips a canvas bag
stuffed with cotton. Fake dollars
line the floor. *Look serious,*
the photographer said. Two years later,
this boy crashed, his body
dead and mangled through windshield.
But that day, he was told, *Look*

like a thief. He holds
a dollar-sign bag to his chest.

That day, this boy
and I rode an old wooden coaster
and we didn't even yell
at the drop.

I once read about a woman
who could no longer feel
her stomach flip. She wanted it back—
that lightness,
that air-jolt on rides,

or driving cars
so quick over hills.

NEIGHBORS

Somewhere, in this building, a baby is crying.
Can you hear that? I ask you. I wake you at night.

One time, I heard that sound in the woods
behind my parent's house. You said, maybe a fox,

maybe a rabbit in distress. *Did it sound like a woman
screaming?* you asked. My cat's cries sound human.

Six hours he wailed after I picked him up, brought him
home in the car to Chicago. Some people

dislike cats, babies. I think I might love
someone kind. I don't know the neighbors.

Somewhere, in this building, a woman is screaming.
My cat perks his ear toward the sound. *Can you hear that?*

I ask you. I wake you at night.

HURON

In Au Gres, kids still run
along the rocky shore of the limestone
point through mud-splash
and they throw sticks at a speedboat.
The sticks fall short,
way out from the hull.

Walrus bone and prehistoric
human remains were found near
this water. Once-plentiful sturgeon
tomahawked in lake shallows.

The settlers once found
large hard maples tapped
by Ojibwa for hundreds of years.

This was lumbering country
and for house-raising, people
came from miles around.
The fiddlers and callers
got people to dance.

They sent logs of old growth
down the river. The men
hunted bear for their stew.

The first switchboard in town
was made of bottles, old bones,
little scraps of iron.

LINEAR FOREIGN BODIES

is what the invoice said
after my cat's surgery
to remove the elastics
he'd swallowed and when the vet
cut him open she said his intestines
were the smelliest she'd ever
known and I ask my cat to never
eat elastics again but we ask
too much of pets and people
so much of each other   please
buy raffle tickets my children's
popcorn we need baked goods
my registry is available
online everything I want
is there and I look for strangers
I tell them my secrets because
even in times like these I
can't stop there are noodles to
boil places that need me places
I go to everyday the other day
I became convinced I smelled bad
asked my friend do I smell bad   please
tell me I am certain this aloneness
is leaking out like sweat
and can you smell it
can you tell the way I breathe
dress think smile is different when
my life changed I was wearing a T-shirt
with a loon on it and no bra   when I'm really
sad missing people I dress up wear
earrings and when my cat uncurls
stands on the bed stretches and walks
away I put my nose to that warmed
crater-space his body left

WHITE-NOSE SYNDROME

i.

I tell you how in two decades
all the common bats may die out,
their muzzles, wings, ears marked
with white fungus, how they sicken
in their dark, cool caves.
You tell me there are other animals.
But what about entire colonies of bats—
97 percent gone in one winter
and three percent springtime stirring,
quietly alive?

ii.

I tell you about living
in France. And can you remember
my frustration, unable
to converse? The way people spoke to me
as if to a child. I tell you about dinner,
when a friend's three-year-old son jumped
at the table, holding his fork like a spear.
Ma peau va craquer? he asked, suddenly
worried his skin might split as his body grows.
It will grow, too, his mother assured. *Ça va
pousser, aussi.*

iii.

Do you remember, near the end,
going to the apple orchard?
I wanted to pick apples with you
and eat them straight from the tree.
It was almost a date. We stomped
on rotting fruit in the grass.

PROGRESS WITHOUT END

—Pullman company motto

Pullman interiors—salons
for luxury, overland travelers.
Gourmet food, leather chairs,
chandeliers. In Chicago, Pullman
means neighborhood, railcar,
industry. Pullman, Illinois
was a model corporate town.
Spotters were hired to report
those who strayed from company
policy. George Pullman worried
angry laborers would vandalize
his grave after death.

In Guatemala, the *pullman*
was the bus full of boys
with machetes, women
selling mango. In Guatemala,
the chicken buses—old
American schoolbuses redone
and charging through mountains
in garish paint, blasting music.

On the bus, before school,
I used to wait outside
in the early-morning dark,
for the doors to open,
for days to begin.
I wonder where that ghost bus
ended up—careening
around curves, spitting diesel. Full
of bodies and noise.

A website calls itself
The Pullman Project, catalogs
the life of Pullman-made
service cars, from the first
called Jamestown in 1907
to the last in 1958. The last
named Dreamland. A database
of cars ending up as restaurants,
exhibits, as scrap.

ABANDONED PLACES

I move to Georgia
and a new friend can't find
a place to get married, to celebrate.
All this land scares her with its
present and haunt hate
its tragedy everywhere and
everywhere.

INTERVIEW PRACTICE

Where do you see yourself in five years?

> Leadership. Taking responsibility. Something about
> working with others.

What is your greatest strength?

> Quality akin to perfectionism. Details explaining
> how strength can equal weakness.
> A funny anecdote about photocopying
> entire novels. How I file the pages by chapter.

What are your obsessions?

> Spontaneous combustions. I watch documentaries. I
> remember the cover image of one—a faded yellow
> armchair. The black round imprint of burn.
>
> Sinking ships.

Are you lucky?

> I never cry while watching moths die. I never get lost
> on the way to the post office.

Describe your career timeline.

> In college, my geology professor lectured on "The
> Timeline of the Far Future." He explained the ways the
> world could die. I imagine new Ice Ages, rising seas,
> exploding suns.

Have you faced adversity?

> I am not drained. I never wander at lunch and forget to
> come back. I never imagine
> the time we laughed in the butterfly garden, I never
> think about placing chestnuts in his outstretched palm.

Tell me about yourself.

> Yesterday, I swear a hawk followed me home. I
> am a person hawks follow home (maybe).
> In fifth grade, I collected rocks. I liked to examine
> the pyrite. I admired the ways
> it wasn't gold.

What do you fear?

> The removal
> of mountains. A joke about
> telemarketers, missing big games.

What do you do when
you're disappointed/
sad/stressed?

> Details about planning
> a future. Walks
> to nowhere. Something
> about wishing, but not believing
> in prayer. Say
> I strive for tradition. Insist
> I'm made for this work.

MINOR PLANETS

The Cererian surface is a mixture
of water-ice, carbonates, and clays.
Discovered in 1801 and classified as a planet
for fifty years, Ceres is a rock-ice body
almost 600 miles across—the largest
asteroid in the inner solar system.

Giuseppe Piazzi discovered Ceres
on New Year's Day over two hundred
years ago. The element cerium was named
after the then-planet, which was named
after the Roman goddess of agriculture,
of harvest, of motherly love. The word
cereal comes from her: a god of grains.

We didn't eat breakfast every morning
but we were going to call
our future son after both our grandfathers.
Drunk at your best friend's wedding, you wrote:
Walter on a chalkboard from across a crowded room.

My grandfather went by Wally, was named
for his father. In 1922, it was the fifteenth
most popular name for boys.

On November 6, 1999 at the Lime Creek
Observatory in Nebraska, Robert Linderholm
named a new main-belt minor planet
after Louis Franklin Lederer, a man described
as *an American businessman and inventor*

of the 20th and 21st centuries. At first, I thought
he'd invented centuries themselves.

Lederer holds four patents for sample collectors
and flow meters. I see these men hovering near
a telescope in Nebraska, hunched in concentration
over research, careful plans.

ALMS FOR THE BIRDS

What is ceremony? It's day in,
day out. It's the feeding
in the morning. It's breath
still leaving you. What is sky
burial? It's ritual. Funerary
Tibetan practice—leave the loved
one on a mountain. Piece
by piece, let vultures take
a death away. Sometimes I want
time to pass. This is the watch
I wear each day. This is tea
I drink in the evening. There
is the neighbor, the mother,
the friend. Point out strange,
familiar signs. How is it—
the days demand more,
demand less? I'll pause
here. What is it like to want loss
picked clean?

NEEDS ASSESSMENT

All I knew was that there were millions of wild animals loose on the plains and I needed money.

—Frank H. Mayer,
The Buffalo Harvest

Across the country, a girl disappears,
            her parents desperately
      speaking to cameras. Somewhere a man walks out

of his home, never to return. In a remote region
            of Siberia, a family hunts
      animals by chasing them until the prey

crumples with exhaustion. In a campus museum
            exhibit, a mangy cat head
      sits preserved in a jar. Sometimes all we know

is what we seem to need. In my office,
            we implement new software to manage
      our customers. *I don't have inventory privileges,*

one colleague complains. Meanwhile,
            in Brazil, a garbage picker finds an infant
      in the trash. As a child, the glow-in-the-dark stars

on my ceiling were at least reminders of actual sky.
            While visiting home, I overhear my father,
      on a business call, say to a subordinate,

What are you trying to solve? A man I once tried
            to date said he started new companies
      only to pass the time. On a pilgrimage

you must look for something. One time a friend
        saw a man run his bloody hands along metal bars
    on the subway. One time I overheard a teenager

say to his girlfriend, *Show me your jugular.* There are portents
        everywhere. At work, we've stopped meeting in person.
    We chat from our cubes, all our phones set to speaker.

Walking the carpeted hallways offers a professional
        chorus of voices. In college, my dance teacher
    would show rare black-and-white footage of dancers,

the movement clouded. She would hop about the room,
        demonstrating signature style,
    movement vocabulary. Sometimes I dream

I am back in France searching for someone
        faceless, unknown. I walk down cobblestone steps.
    When I wake, all I remember are wires.

Notes

Epigraphs from "Millions," "How to Care for Buffalo Horns," and "Needs Assessment" come from *The Buffalo Harvest* by Frank H. Mayer (with Charles B. Roth). The text chronicles Mayer's experience as a buffalo hunter in the American West in the 1870s.

The last two lines of "Abandoned Places" are taken from an anonymous prompt from a writer in Debra Marquart's poetry workshop at Iowa State University, spring 2014.

"Adapted" borrows language and information from the book review "The horses we rode in on" from *The Globe and Mail*, August 19, 2006.

"To Disappear in Michigan" borrows language from the article "Does an 'Extinct' Cat Prowl in Michigan? Experts Puzzle over an Elusive Big Cat" by Bob Butz, from the National Wildlife Federation website, October 1, 2003.

"My Dad's Brother Called Every Year for Five Years Then Disappeared" borrows language from the article "Revealed: Human feet that washed up on Pacific coast were from people who committed suicide—and were wearing buoyant rubber-soled shoes" by Daniel Bates from the *Daily Mail*, March 4, 2004.

In "New Year," the quote from Wilbur Wright is a statement he allegedly once gave to reporters.

"Frontier Airlines" takes a line and inspiration from "Fork with Two Tines Pushed Together" by Nick Lantz, from *How to Dance while the Roof Caves In*.

"The Center of the Earth is a Little Off Kilter" takes its title from a *New York Times* article from September 24, 2012.

"Huron" takes information from local historical accounts printed up and housed in the Au Gres Public Library.

Instructions from "How to Adjust to Time Zones," "How to Care for Buffalo Horns," and "How to Measure the Weight of Snow" are taken from eHow.com articles.

Iowa Poetry Prize and
Edwin Ford Piper Poetry Award Winners

1987   Elton Glaser, *Tropical Depressions*
Michael Pettit, *Cardinal Points*

1988   Bill Knott, *Outremer*
Mary Ruefle, *The Adamant*

1989   Conrad Hilberry, *Sorting the Smoke*
Terese Svoboda, *Laughing Africa*

1990   Philip Dacey, *Night Shift at the Crucifix Factory*
Lynda Hull, *Star Ledger*

1991   Greg Pape, *Sunflower Facing the Sun*
Walter Pavlich, *Running near the End of the World*

1992   Lola Haskins, *Hunger*
Katherine Soniat, *A Shared Life*

1993   Tom Andrews, *The Hemophiliac's Motorcycle*
Michael Heffernan, *Love's Answer*
John Wood, *In Primary Light*

1994   James McKean, *Tree of Heaven*
Bin Ramke, *Massacre of the Innocents*
Ed Roberson, *Voices Cast Out to Talk Us In*

1995   Ralph Burns, *Swamp Candles*
Maureen Seaton, *Furious Cooking*

1996   Pamela Alexander, *Inland*
Gary Gildner, *The Bunker in the Parsley Fields*
John Wood, *The Gates of the Elect Kingdom*

1997   Brendan Galvin, *Hotel Malabar*
          Leslie Ullman, *Slow Work through Sand*

1998   Kathleen Peirce, *The Oval Hour*
          Bin Ramke, *Wake*
          Cole Swensen, *Try*

1999   Larissa Szporluk, *Isolato*
          Liz Waldner, *A Point Is That Which Has No Part*

2000   Mary Leader, *The Penultimate Suitor*

2001   Joanna Goodman, *Trace of One*
          Karen Volkman, *Spar*

2002   Lesle Lewis, *Small Boat*
          Peter Jay Shippy, *Thieves' Latin*

2003   Michele Glazer, *Aggregate of Disturbances*
          Dainis Hazners, *(some of) The Adventures of Carlyle,*
             My Imaginary Friend

2004   Megan Johnson, *The Waiting*
          Susan Wheeler, *Ledger*

2005   Emily Rosko, *Raw Goods Inventory*
          Joshua Marie Wilkinson, *Lug Your Careless Body out*
             of the Careful Dusk

2006   Elizabeth Hughey, *Sunday Houses the Sunday House*
          Sarah Vap, *American Spikenard*

2008   Andrew Michael Roberts, *something has to happen next*
          Zach Savich, *Full Catastrophe Living*

2009   Samuel Amadon, *Like a Sea*
          Molly Brodak, *A Little Middle of the Night*

2010   Julie Hanson, *Unbeknownst*
          L. S. Klatt, *Cloud of Ink*